MORE
Little Nuns

cartoons by
Joe Lane

compiled by
Eileen O'Hayer

published by About Comics, Camarillo, California

More Little Nuns
Originally published by *Extension Magazine*, 1951
About Comics edition published April, 2018

Customized editions available

Send all queries to questions@aboutcomics.com

"*Give me five minutes in that backfield and I'd put that game on ice.*"

"How many?"

"One!"

"She spent five years in the WACS before coming here!"

"Don't touch her, Mike . . . she's consecrated . . . use the shovel!"

"My third graders do much better."

"Good conduct? Not you, Willie!"

"*Ah, good Sister, could you aid and abet one who has fulfilled his class prophecy of being the one least likely to succeed?*"

"Tow that wreck out of here!"

"Touche!"

"Does this look cleaner now?"

"We need honest watchers at the polls. . . . Should we ask them?"

"Twenty-four pairs of bobby sox?"

"Trick or treat!"

"Trick or treat!"

"Sister's taking me to match wits with the Principal."

LANE

*"Thank God they're tucked in safely ... I was worried sick
about them at the picnic!"*

"*Chartreuse thread, anyone?*"

"Oh, no trouble, officer—we're just waiting 'till our hour is up."

"Anything you care to donate is deductible on your income tax."

"Nice, juicy hash . . . smothered with leftovers."

"Can I borrow the catcher's mask, Sister?"

"Eight nuns and one novice . . . put down eight and a half, Al."

"Now relax, children, nothing to be afraid of."

"We'll save you from those rustlers, Sister!"

"*This way, but please keep silence. . . . The Sisters are at prayer.*"

LANE

"Our sewing teacher."

"This car needs overhauling, Sister Bertha.
It keeps dragging in the rear."

"You may eat that taffy apple when the bell rings for lunch."

"When can we have another party, Sister?"

"Not enough room on the blackboard, Sister."

"*Stand in the corner and say three Hail Marys.*"

"*I can't. I only know one.*"

"*Now let me tell you the cute things he does in class!*"

"Sister'll be all right—had her first class today!"

"Father's just back from giving a mission in Texas."

"And now we leave these hallowed halls of learning to face the grim realities of the outside world."

"Security regulations forbid me to divulge any information."

"Nothing, thanks . . . just looking."

"The varmints went that-a-way!"

"The diner's open."

"The pastor would like to borrow his clubs this afternoon."

"I wonder if she's going to tell Father she took my water pistol!"

"Say hello to Sister."

Get all our little books of Joe Lane's little nuns

Our Little Nuns
More Little Nuns
Nuns So Lovable
Vale of Dears
Yes, Sister! No, Sister!

or get

The Big Book of Nun Cartoons
a lifetime supply all in one volume!

Look for them where you got this book,
or visit www.AboutComics.com

Classic Cartoon Collections!

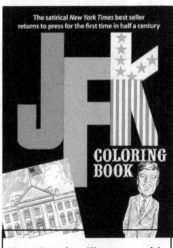

THE WORKS OF
CHARLES M. SCHULZ